THE NINTH-GRADE GUIDE FOR INVOLVED PARENTS

ELLEN SHRAGER

Illustrated by Abby Bosley and Anthony T. Shelton, Sr.

TEACHER VOICE PUBLISHING
P.O. BOX 446
VILLANOVA, PA 19085

COPYRIGHT © 2012 BY ELLEN SHRAGER

All rights reserved. No part of this book may be reproduced in any form or by any electronic or mechanical means, including information storage and retrieval systems, without permission in writing from the publisher, except by a reviewer, who may quote brief passages in a review.

For information about special discounts for bulk purchases, please contact Teacher Voice Publishing at 1-610-355-0553 or teachervoicepublishing@comcast.net.

Illustrated by Abby Bosley and Anthony T. Shelton, Sr.

MANUFACTURED IN THE UNITED STATES OF AMERICA
14 13 12 11 10   2 3 4 5

Library of Congress Control Number: 2010932687

ISBN 978-0-9793200-2-6

To

all the parents out there who want to do the right thing and listen to the village, but just need some encouragement to do it; may this be that encouragement.

and to Anne, Dee, George, John, and Mary for sharing their children with me.

CONTENTS

Acknowledgments vii
Introduction ix

NINTH-GRADE BEHAVIORS AND THE COMMON APPLICATION

Integrity and Cheating 3
The Myth of Extracurricular Activities 13
Good Grades versus Disciplined Work Habits 17
Reaction to Setbacks 23
Initiative and Independence 30
Self-Confidence 34
Respect Accorded by Faculty 44
Concern for Others 53
Conclusion 58

APPENDICES

Appendix 1 – Habits Students Need 62
Appendix 2 – The Myth of the Heavy Backpack 76
Appendix 3 – Avoiding Dress Code Violations 78
Appendix 4 – Making the Transition to a New Building ... 80
Appendix 5 – Summer Suggestions 82
Appendix 6 – Institutions Accepting the Common App ... 84
References 99
About the Author 101

ACKNOWLEDGMENTS

I'd like to thank my friends and family for sharing their journey through parenting with me:

Suzanne and Tom Stone
Dee Sharp and Stan Jones
Anne and Dick Howe
John and Michelle Bernard
Donna Pietropaolo, Patricia and George Bernard
Mary and Art Hull
Holly and Jim Frank   Sue and Marc Gerwertz
Janet and Dave Hurlbrink   Lisa and John Hvizda
Jenna, Jon, Laura, and Ben Howe
Abby and Jack Waterstreet   Lee and Tim Ames
Donna and Keith Purkey   Stephanie and Doug Grande
Linda Bradley and Jean Farrell

A special thanks to Katy Lemon of the Common Application, Inc. for facilitating permission to use their forms.

My friend, Barb, spent countless hours on the manuscript. Her editing skills are amazing and her friendship, priceless. Thanks, Barb.

While presenting at ASCA, two professional school counselors urged me to spend my summer re-writing my seventh-grade guide for incoming ninth graders. Thanks to Rick Sorrels and Bonnie Buice Allison for their "guidance."

My sister Anne is able to listen to my stories, help me to process the problems, and refine my responses. She makes me a better teacher, a better colleague, and a better person. For the record, she is right only 99.8 percent of the time.

Although there are many fingerprints all over this book, I alone am responsible for any errors.

Introduction

Technology has forever changed parenting.

Previous generations of parents* would turn to their own parents for advice on how to navigate the choppy waters of raising adolescents. But today's grandparents have no experience to share on how to handle cyber-bullying, how to appropriately respond to grades posted online, how to appropriately limit texting, or how to undo an adolescent mistake forever embedded on the Internet.

Today's involved parents are on their own. Most are understandably fearful that one misstep may cause permanent damage or at the very least cause their child to miss out on a coveted college acceptance. These parents create a "trophy student" and evaluate their parenting skills based on the quality of their child's college acceptances.

They are shortsighted for two reasons.

First, the retention rate of college freshmen returning as sophomores to the same four-year institution is reported to be approximately 76 percent in the United States: one in four students don't return! Second, these "trophy students" are now perceived as high-maintenance employees in the workforce. These

---

*As a literary device, I use "parent" and "parents" to include guardians and family members other than parents who are raising our students.

INTRODUCTION

employees are unable to independently meet deadlines without their managers' reminders.

To use a football metaphor, these shortsighted parents mistakenly stopped at the 20-yard line and congratulated themselves on a job well done without realizing the next twenty yards would determine the quality of their child's *adult* life.

These misguided parents are afraid of what will happen to their children if they are not accepted to the "right" college when they should be afraid of what will happen if their children can't self-regulate, can't be honest with them, or can't accept natural consequences.

By focusing merely on the college acceptance, in my opinion, many of today's involved parents overshoot their role of "protective manager" to their elementary school children and fail to make the timely transition to their role of "coach" to their adolescents.

By the time the parents realize what they should have been doing, they have missed the grace period when grades and consequences do not impact college applications and teacher evaluations: sixth, seventh and eighth grade.

Middle school was the perfect time to let your child make mistakes. That willingness to let your child falter may have gone against your instinct to help create success, but it would pay dividends in your

INTRODUCTION

child's future: scoring well on a teacher evaluation for college applications, staying in college, and keeping a job upon graduation.

What if you missed this grace period and your child is now entering ninth grade?

All is not lost, but many parents mistakenly focus on just the two technical factors that contribute to the importance of ninth grade: class rank and GPA.

These misguided parents overlook the third factor, the "soft skills" evaluated on the teacher evaluation of the Common Application.

Do you know about the Common Application?

If not, that is understandable. Perhaps one of the biggest differences between when you applied to college and when your child will apply to college is that approximately 500 colleges use the Common Application. Your child fills out one application, the teacher fills out one evaluation, and it is sent to as many colleges as you want or can afford.

With the one application and early decision being a popular choice among seniors, there is little time to apply, learn from your mistakes, adjust, and apply somewhere else. For a list of the colleges and universities accepting the Common Application, go to page 84.

INTRODUCTION

What if the college of your choice doesn't use the Common Application? Professional high school counselors tell me that many colleges and universities using their own forms strongly resemble the form for the Common Application.

Now that you know about the Common Application, Let's examine the three factors that contribute to the importance of ninth grade: class rank, GPA, and teacher evaluation on the Common Application.

1. **Class Rank.** Day one of ninth grade is when the school starts tracking your child's class rank compared to all of the other students in his or her class. It is considered a better indicator to college admissions of how your child performs during this age of alleged grade inflation. Some schools have discontinued this practice, check with your own school.

2. **GPA.** Students applying for colleges during the beginning of their senior year forward the transcript from ninth to eleventh in their preliminary application.

   GPA is calculated by multiplying the grade your child earned by the 'weight' of the course. Educate yourself about the different weights of the courses else you may be surprised as was one mother whose ninth-grade daughter earned an "A" in every class she took at the *accelerated* level. The surprise? There are

INTRODUCTION

four levels in her building, Academic, Accelerated, Honors and AP. The students with "A"s in Honors automatically had higher GPAs then her daughter in Accelerated. Her daughter has a 4.0 average but others have a 5.0 average. She did some investigating with the school counselor and learned that her daughter was actually in the bottom third of her class while her mother was under the impression she was in the top ten percent. Make sure you understand how your school values its different courses, and determine the best fit for your child.

If your child has not learned the right habits to earn grades that accurately reflect his or her ability, then ninth grade is the perfect time to help your child to acquire these habits. Even if it takes a few quarters to see the results of acquiring these habits on the report card, the Common Application and most colleges and universities not using the Common Application provide the opportunity for the student to explain how he or she overcame a setback. For example, the Common Application states: **"Additional Information:** If there is any additional information you'd like to provide regarding special circumstances, additional qualifications, etc., please do so in the space below or on an attached sheet."

INTRODUCTION

3. **Teacher Evaluation.** Your child will be asking the high school teachers for letters of recommendation and for a completed teacher evaluation for the Common Application. It is better if this information is from a teacher who has known your child for a while and not just the first few months of senior year. Usually a student chooses a teacher from the junior year and who may also be teaching an upper-level course during the senior year. What does the Common Application ask the teacher? First, they want to know how long the teacher has known the student and in what context. Second, they want the first words that come to the teacher's mind to describe the student. Third, they ask for a list of the course**s** the teacher taught the student noting the student's year in school and level of course difficulty.

So, the good news is that if you haven't addressed some of the behaviors that we are about to explore, you can still address and correct them now, in ninth grade, before your child acts them out in front of the teacher who will be writing the teacher evaluation.

How do I know?

INTRODUCTION

I used to work in the admissions office at Boston College. Later, I taught high school and, as the class advisor, became privy to how scholarships, letters of recommendations, and awards are bestowed on our seniors. Currently I teach in a large junior high.

Over the course of my teaching career, I have taught more than 3,000 adolescents. I keep in contact with and follow many of my former students. I am privy to a lot that goes on with them and with my own large extended family and friends.

The insight gained from these relationships and from my own teaching experience is shared in my book **Teacher Dialogues.** From Wenatchee, Washington, to Portland, Maine, I train teachers to guide parents to truly help their children.

As I visit different schools for teacher training, I require an advance list of the biggest employers in the area and the parents' list of desirable colleges. I contact the colleges, and based on my prior work experience in the admissions office and my assurance that I have no child trying to gain admission, I ask key questions and receive frank answers from the admissions counselors. I also contact the human resource offices at the largest employers and ask them about their hiring and firing practices. I link behaviors high school teachers observe to behaviors that future employers desire. I share this information with teachers so that they can help parents.

INTRODUCTION

Now, I am sharing it directly with parents because many parents are crafting their child's experiences based on parental fears and illusions rather than today's college admission reality. Why do today's parents do this?

Societal Changes Influence Parenting

Society has changed since I first started teaching, and many parental reactions are a logical consequence of these societal changes. In my opinion, the top three changes in society that result in parental fear are:

1. With more options for women, many couples delayed starting a family and had difficulty creating a family. Growing up as baby boomers, my friends and I frequently acquired unplanned siblings; in contrast, my brother-in-law views the odds of his daughter's birth taking place as one in a million. Parents with fewer children may be more protective than parents with more children.

2. The media stokes parental fears and paranoia about child safety, creating a society of obsessive observers who watch their children over the Internet, on the nanny cam, and even when the child is away at camp or overseas. Once the child leaves elementary school and the opportunity for parental involvement in the building disappears, some parents struggle with having a child out of their reach during the day.

INTRODUCTION

The events of 9/11 have heightened our sense of vulnerability in this country, making parents understandably more fearful.

3. High-stakes testing and job outsourcing stoke the fear of increased competition, compelling some parents to emphasize grades, not learning. They are concerned that the glut of people with college degrees means that many college graduates will not find jobs with the benefit of health insurance. My parents believed that as long as we went to college and got a good liberal arts education, we would be able to provide for ourselves. Today's parents believe that if children don't go to the right college and the right grad school, they will never find a job and never match the lifestyle in which they were raised.

There are other factors as well. For instance, when both parents work and spend only a few hours a day with their child, they may be motivated to make those few hours pleasant and conflict-free.

My father also felt that time with his loved ones was very precious. He was drafted into WWII at the age of twenty-seven and didn't start a family until later in life. He described parenthood as cutting out your own heart and putting it in the careless hand of a toddler who could easily, unintentionally break it. He said

INTRODUCTION

that once you have children, your day could only be as good as one of your children's worst moments.

In spite of my father's tenderness for us, he would never understand today's TV shows that depict children running the house and parents afraid and unwilling to correct them—or the real-life families that these shows are based on.

Instead, my father believed that correcting children is an act of love and a sacred obligation; the parent-child bond will be strengthened, not diminished, by correction. This is in stark contrast to one of my colleagues, who also became a father later in life. He told me that he doesn't believe in time-outs or consequences for his sons because it hurts too much. In spite of being a middle-school teacher for twenty-five years, he just can't do it.

"Kids Rule"

While historically parents have always feared losing their child to death, some of today's parents have so much vested in so few children that they carry the burden of an additional fear: some parents fear losing

INTRODUCTION

their child's companionship more than they fear losing their jobs or divorcing. As a result, they won't enforce consequences because they are terrified that their child's temporary frustrations and anger at being held accountable will result in rejection.

Some parents fear ultimately losing their child's approval. This thought is so devastating to them, that when their children do make mistakes, *and it is impossible for adolescents not to make mistakes*, these parents refuse to believe the truth, so that they don't have to face the issue. Instead, they spin illusions to justify the disconnect with reality. They deprive their child of the chance to convert a mistake into a learning experience, and the results will be disappointingly obvious when it comes time to fill out college applications and request teacher evaluations.

Our Beloved Children

When did you know in your heart that you wanted to become a parent?

I like to ask people this question. Among my circle of friends and family, it frequently happens after the birth of someone else's baby, or after attending a four-year-old's ballet recital, or after an amazing conversation with someone's tyke.

I have yet to hear "Well, I was shopping in the mall and saw a bunch of thirteen-year-olds hanging out and after noticing the way they dressed and wore

INTRODUCTION

makeup, and the tone of voice they used with one another, I said to myself, 'Hot dang, I need to get me one of those.'"

Why? Because with today's technology, adolescents have access to information unlike previous generations. The role of parenting has shifted from gradually exposing the world to children to actively guarding children from too much exposure to inappropriate ideas as close to their children as their cell phones.

Did I mention I'll be 14 next week?

There is one caveat. While some students are physically maturing at younger ages, there remains a solid small group of students in ninth grade who are "late-bloomers" for a variety of reasons (e.g., the increasing number of "preemies" or the increasing number of diagnosed and non-diagnosed students on the autism spectrum). When I speak of ninth graders,

INTRODUCTION

I am excluding that 10 percent that have a history of developmental delay, rather I am talking about typical ninth graders, who usually are not the poster children to entice couples to become parents.

I have taught every grade from middle school to the second year of college and ninth grade offers its own delights and pitfalls.

Adolescent Behavior

I don't know if it is hormones, the challenges of becoming a teenager, or something else, but there is a definite shift as ninth graders seek more approval from peers than from parents or teachers.

I warn parents that they will not recognize some of the behaviors that their child will most likely demonstrate. One parent compared it to an alien intermittently taking over her precious child's mind with no warning and no set schedule. For example:

- ♥ Independent thinkers suddenly put their own sense of right or wrong in their backpack and care more about what others think.

- ♥ A student who comes home and tells you everything about her day deftly omits some events that you only discover from other sources.

INTRODUCTION

- ♥ A pacifist will suddenly become addicted to the violent video game that all of his friends are playing.

- ♥ A student's lifelong friendship will be ditched overnight to enhance his or her own status with "cooler" students.

- ♥ Students will seek out their own identity with clothing, hairstyles, and body image, and start choosing partners to date.

Most parents understand these examples; at this point, you may be nodding your head in agreement at the classic adolescent behavior that comes with the territory.

But, other behaviors surprise parents so much that the head nodding stops. Most parents are stunned by the list that I have culled from thousands of teachers from all fifty states and Canada attending my presentations.

These teachers want parents to know:

- ♥ This is the year your child may manipulate adults against one another, whether it be parent against teacher, parent against parent, grandparent against parent.

- ♥ This is the year your child may omit parts of the truth as a passive lie to you.

- ♥ This is the year your previously honest child may directly lie to you.

INTRODUCTION

- This is the year your previously honest child may be caught cheating on a quiz or test.
- This is the year your child may submit a project that is pure plagiarism off the Internet.
- This is the year that your child may avoid consequences by using excuses like "I didn't know" or "That teacher doesn't like me."
- This is the year your previously kind child does something unrecognizably cruel to another child, even a former good friend.
- This is the year parents fully realize the extent that Facebook, texting, e-mail, and video games distract students from studying.
- This is the year students will feel more pressure as these grades will go on the college transcript and the clock starts ticking for class rank.
- This is the year they will want to appear older to impress upper classmen.
- This is the year students over-commit to activities and they struggle to keep balance.
- This is the year your child may act out problems and deviant behavior with electronic technology, such as cyber-bullying for girls and porn fascination for boys.

INTRODUCTION

- ♥ This is the year friendship changes and older boys start showing an interest in ninth-grade girls.
- ♥ This is the year your child may deeply disappoint you.

Most first-time parents to an adolescent are shocked by this list. Perhaps you are too. Typically, most parents begin to process this list by thinking about their child's friends and neighbors and can begin to picture specific children doing a few of these things.

Most parents believe in their heart that it won't be their child, just someone else's child. As one mother explained to me, "Our son began to speak at nine months. He has always been so verbal that we thought that we would just talk him through adolescence without having to experience it—boy, were we wrong!"

The good news is that in most schools the ninth-grade teachers are not the ones to complete the teacher evaluations for college applications. Your child may try out some undesirable behaviors during ninth grade, and you will have the opportunity to process these occurrences with them. Viewed through the lens that this is typical behavior and not a reflection of your parenting, you can correct your child so that the behavior is addressed and disappears before your

INTRODUCTION

child is in the class of the teacher who will write a teacher evaluation.

For the rest of this book we will:

- ♥ Relate ninth-grade behaviors to the Common Application.
- ♥ Discuss how to talk to your adolescent when these behaviors arise in such a way that you get to the heart of the matter.
- ♥ Examine some of the habits your child should be acquiring.
- ♥ Review when to manage, when to coach, and how to train your ninth grader to appropriately negotiate with teachers.

NINTH-GRADE BEHAVIORS

AND

THE COMMON APPLICATION

Parents and teachers shouldn't be judged on the presence or absence of problems, but on how they respond to them.

Integrity and Cheating

The book, Student Cheating and Plagiarism in the Internet Era: A Wake-Up Call by Ann Lathrop and Kathleen Foss (2007) cites these statistics:

- ♥ 80% of high school students admit to cheating.
- ♥ 95% of students who cheat say they don't get caught.
- ♥ 34% say their parents never talk to them about cheating.

The statistic that approximately one-third of parents never talk to students about cheating corresponds with my experience.

One parent, a fellow teacher married to another teacher, told me in disbelief, "We asked our son why he had the cheat sheet out for your quiz and he said, 'Because you told me if I wanted to play baseball I had to get good grades no matter what!' We told him *that didn't mean cheating,* and he replied 'you never said that.' Can you believe this? He is the son of two teachers—we never thought we had to spell this out to him!"

Another mom told me, when I saw her daughter take a student's homework out of his backpack and start copying (unbeknownst to the student who had done the work) "Mrs. Shrager, I just don't recognize that as

INTEGRITY AND CHEATING

being one of my daughter's behaviors because her father and I never taught her to do that!"

When told that your child cheated on a test, or copied someone else's homework, your first instinct will be, "There are two sides to every story." While this approach may be correct when an issue arises between two elementary school students, teachers and adolescent students are not equals. You cannot take the same approach. With adolescence, there is (1) reality as observed by the teacher and (2) an adolescent trying to avoid a consequence for a bad choice or an impulsive action. By inviting the student to be equal to the teacher, you are setting your child up to lie to you and to cling to that lie.

This is dangerous. Your child needs to learn that he or she will survive when you discover these adolescent mistakes and that both of you will quickly get past it.

If your child does not learn from these experiences that you both will survive the bad choices, your child

THE NINTH-GRADE GUIDE FOR INVOLVED PARENTS

may be reluctant to share information about bad choices with you in time for you to help them. For example, if he or she is about to get into a car with someone drinking, or isn't about to graduate, *he or she may make a fatal choice because of the lack of practice of telling you disappointing news and lack of learning that you both will survive it.*

Here's an example that shows the different results that can occur from two different ways of handling the same problem.

Two girls, "Kate" and "Jen," cheated on a quiz in my class. They both admitted that Kate had asked Jen for two answers and that Jen had supplied them, and in return, asked for a different answer. I told them that this was a disappointment and that both would receive a zero for their quiz grade. I also gave the girls two days to bring me a note from their parents stating that they were aware of the cheating incident.

Jen's dad wrote that he was amazed that this had happened. He and his daughter discussed why she couldn't say "no" to her friend even when she knew it was wrong, and why she couldn't just leave one answer blank.

Jen and her dad had a difficult-but great-heart-to-heart talk about peer pressure. She offered to send me an apology note as well, and her dad was proud of that. A month later, another student in the class was

INTEGRITY AND CHEATING

caught cheating and I heard Jen tell him, "Go ahead, and do what she says. It is so much better once your parents know."

On the other hand, Kate's mom could not hear the truth. She wrote me back that I was mistaken. She said her child wouldn't cheat and that they were just chatting during the quiz, forgetting that they couldn't talk.

This parent and child could not get to a point of honesty. The daughter learned that her mother couldn't handle the truth. As well, they both missed the chance to discuss whether Kate's participation in numerous sports teams outside school might have prevented her from studying. A few months later, she was ineligible to play sports because of her low grades in other classes.

From this experience, I learned to listen to a parent's language: when a parent is shrouded in illusion, rather than grounded in reality, the parent refers to "my child" and not to the student by name. It indicates that the parent is unwilling to see the child as a good, albeit imperfect, individual. Rather, the parent is marketing a "my child" package as a scorecard of his or her parenting skills.

THE NINTH-GRADE GUIDE FOR INVOLVED PARENTS

I spoke with Kate's mother a while later, when Kate was caught copying someone's homework. Mom was still bitter about "my" previous mistake. I once again tried to explain that her daughter was a good person, that I am very fond of her and of my other students, but that I have seen that some children do not feel able to tell their parents about a dangerous situation, and I wouldn't want to see it happen to such a fine person.

Her mother smugly told me, "No worries, I told her that she could always tell me anything—she could always call me to come get her if someone is driving while under the influence, no problem." Meanwhile, Kate continued to struggle in school and was dropped from the team.

Children will struggle to share an unpleasant truth when their parents cling to an illusion that they have taken care of this problem.

What do you think? Which girl, Jen or Kate, would most likely reach out to her parent with a problem in the future?

(The evening after I wrote these words, I read an article in my local paper about a boy receiving his **second** ticket for driving violations. According to the article, he felt he just could not go home and tell his parents; instead he committed suicide.)

Now let's take this one step further. Let's imagine what may happen down the road when both girls apply to colleges.

Let's say that Jen has learned to never exchange answers. Kate still cheats as a strategy for getting good grades. They both are applying to colleges that use the Common Application. For a list of colleges that use the Common Application, go to Appendix Six, page 84.

THE NINTH-GRADE GUIDE FOR INVOLVED PARENTS

Look at the teacher evaluation form from the Common Application on the next page. Which student Jen or Kate will merit the higher score for "integrity"?

Time and again I have heard parents and seniors moan about who got into the preferred school. Parents tell me that their child had higher class rank and scores, but someone else was admitted. The parents assume that the other student had some kind of connection.

Maybe, or maybe not! Back in the 90s, a local bank agreed to abide by my decision, as the class advisor, to award a $10,000 yearly scholarship for college to the girl ranked <u>third</u> in her class. I recommended her over the two top students because I had never caught her cheating, she never came in late to class on the day a project was due, and she took the hardest classes. The other two had both cheated in my class as sophomores.

Below is a portion of the Common Application's teacher evaluation.

INTEGRITY AND CHEATING

	Good (above average)	Very good (well above average)	Excellent (top 10%)	Outstanding (top 5%)	One of the top few I've encountered (top 1%)
Academic achievement					
Intellectual promise					
Quality of writing					
Creative, original thought					
Productive class discussion					
Respect accorded by faculty					
Disciplined work habits					
Maturity					
Motivation					
Leadership					
(Integrity)					
Reaction to setbacks					
Concern for others					
Self-confidence					
Initiative, independence					
OVERALL					

© 2011 The Common Application, Inc. Reprinted with permission

THE NINTH-GRADE GUIDE FOR INVOLVED PARENTS

Why is integrity so important that the colleges want the teachers to evaluate the applicant?

With technology, cheating is on the rise. Search the Internet for students using their cell phones to cheat, for students buying completed term papers, and for students expelled for sharing answers on Facebook. You will learn that not only is cheating on the rise, but that parents whose goal was college acceptance at any price may discover how costly it is to retain a lawyer to fight their child's expulsion for cheating.

Unlike public high school, some colleges expel students for cheating. The University of Georgia, the University of Virginia, Central Connecticut State University, and Duke, to name a few, have expelled students in recent years for cheating.

In 2009, Simon Fraser University in Canada instituted a new grade of "FD" for "failed for academic dishonesty." Other universities may follow suit.

If you do not address the issue of cheating and integrity as it arises, your child may not receive the best teacher evaluation, nor be able to eliminate cheating as a time management tool while in college—with disappointing and expensive consequences.

Furthermore, cheating in ninth grade can create problems at home. One student, a boy very active in

INTEGRITY AND CHEATING

our school play, in sports, and in student government, cheated in my class. He waited all weekend to speak to his mother when his father wasn't around. Finally, late Sunday night, he asked his mom to sign a blank piece of paper for "a handwriting assignment in class." He then filled in the rest of the note from the mother explaining she knew all about the cheating incident. The father saw the paper the next morning and confronted his son, making everyone late for work and school.

The father ruefully observed that the family wouldn't have had to go through this drama, which impacted their jobs, if only their son could have told them the truth. The family then went on to set up reasonable limitations on the son's extracurricular activities. In the pursuit of numerous extracurricular activities for the perfect college application, they had over-looked grades and reality, which brings us to the myth of extracurricular activities.

THE NINTH-GRADE GUIDE FOR INVOLVED PARENTS

The Myth of Extracurricular Activities

How can involvement in extracurricular activities possibly be an undesirable behavior? When it deprives a ninth grader of the time needed to learn good study habits.

If your child is in three different activities every day after school in order to have enough activities for the college application, it is time to get a reality check.

How many activities do you think your child needs for the college application for the first three years of high school including summers?

What kinds of activities should they be? If you are thinking "the more, the merrier," you may be working from the paradigm when you applied to college. Let's look at the Common Application.

Including summers and volunteer activities, over the first three years of high school, the Common Application has provided only 7 spaces for extracurricular activities. (see page 14.)

THE MYTH OF EXTRACURRICULAR ACTIVITIES

ACTIVITIES

Extracurricular Please list your principal extracurricular, community, volunteer and family activities and hobbies in the order of their interest to you. Include specific events and/or major accomplishments such as musical instrument played, varsity letters earned, etc. To allow us to focus on the highlights of your activities, please complete this section even if you plan to attach a résumé.

Grade level or post-graduate (PG)				Approximate time spent		When did you participate in the activity?			Positions held, honors won, or letters earned	If applicable, do you plan to participate in college?
9	10	11	12	PG	Hours per week	Weeks per year	School year	Summer		
○	○	○	○	○			○	○		○
Activity										
○	○	○	○	○			○	○		○
Activity										
○	○	○	○	○			○	○		○
Activity										
○	○	○	○	○			○	○		○
Activity										
○	○	○	○	○			○	○		○
Activity										
○	○	○	○	○			○	○		○
Activity										
○	○	○	○	○			○	○		○
Activity										

Work Experience Please list paid jobs you have held during the past three years (including summer employment).

Specific nature of work	Employer	School year	Summer	Approximate dates (mm/yyyy - mm/yyyy)	Hours per week

© 2011 The Common Application, Inc. Reprinted with permission.

THE NINTH-GRADE GUIDE FOR INVOLVED PARENTS

The colleges that I have contacted have told me that they will get their diversity from having students with varied interests—each student does not have to be completely diversified. In fact, they are looking for students who can sustain an interest and take on the role of leadership. Look at the column labeled "Approximate time spent" on the application. Colleges want to know how many hours per week and weeks per year the student has dedicated to the activity.

If your child hasn't done so previously, than ninth grade is the time to try different activities in order to find an interest that will sustain your child through all four years of high school and demonstrate leadership and accomplishment. This activity does not have to necessarily be a school-sponsored activity; if your child is passionate about a community activity or an activity sponsored by his or her place of worship, that activity qualifies for the college application.

While it is tempting to steer your child into an activity that you think would look best on a college application, you really need to follow your child's true passion that will sustain his or her interest. One parent, a scientist, knew she could help her daughter to excel in The Biology Club. She reasoned that if her child were ever going to be pre-med, this would look great on a college application.

THE MYTH OF EXTRACURRICULAR ACTIVITIES

Her daughter dutifully participated in The Biology Club but was enamored with a group opposed to the death penalty. She would put hours into this cause and eventually became the president of this club. Her passion for this activity became one of her college essays and she was accepted early admission into the college of her choice.

Since freshmen's grades do show up on the high school transcript for college, this is the time to discover sustainable interests while maintaining the best scores possible, without cheating to obtain the grades.

The focus on *grades* will not be enough to sustain your child's academic success; instead focus on *good habits and learning*.

Good Grades versus Disciplined Work Habits

Some students have a fairly easy time in elementary school, learning by listening, completing one project at a time, and having one teacher remind students what they need to bring home each afternoon for homework. In elementary school, if a student is absent, work can made up during recess.

When these students reach middle school, they may struggle with taking on the responsibility of making up work after an absence since it is not built into the school day. They may need to stay up all night to focus on one test or one project and to make sure enough work was done to get the "90" that shows up as an A, indiscernible from a "99" on the report card, in many middle schools.

Many parents believe that middle school is all about socialization and as long as the minimally acceptable grades are earned, they don't need to worry. But if students don't develop the habits that will sustain them when the course work invariably becomes more rigorous in high school, the students will fall behind.

Why is the course work more rigorous? Because many middle school students are taught by a team of teachers who imperceptibly balance the workload including projects for them. Many middle schools assign test dates to each department so that students

GOOD GRADES VERSUS DISCIPLINED WORK HABITS

never have more than two tests per day in a major subject. In ninth grade, the tests and projects are no longer sheltered and many students are introduced to cumulative examinations being factored into their semester grade. Homework can help move information from the short-term memory into the long-term memory, improving scores on cumulative exams.

Most ninth graders understand that they need to do a written assignment. Wait, I take that back.

Parents frequently make the mistake of asking their ninth grader, "Do you have any homework tonight?" This is an abstract concept.

Since many students do not fine-tune their abstract thinking until around age fifteen, you need to make it concrete for them by going through each subject with your child i.e., "What do you have for math homework? English? Social studies? Science? Spanish? Reading?"

Students may say "no," pause—"I just have to study for two tests." These students are just focusing on written work to hand in—not connecting to preparing for a test as homework! If you stop listening at "no," you will miss the real answer.

If your child is on block scheduling, he or she may very well think back on the day, decide nothing is due tomorrow, only to discover the next day there *was* homework from two days ago.

THE NINTH-GRADE GUIDE FOR INVOLVED PARENTS

Or if your child only has a class twice a week, he or she may forget that during that class three days ago, the teacher assigned homework that is now due tomorrow.

Furthermore, many ninth graders don't grasp the idea of reviewing each major subject five or ten minutes a night if there is no written homework. But it is important to teach them this habit.

If you want to give your child the competitive edge, establish a time each day to go through the most current notes from each class, learn five words a night in the foreign language class, five definitions in science, five facts in social studies, and five new vocabulary words in English. This habit will sustain your child through high school more than endless activities.

How important are positive habits? Although baby boomers were taught that high IQ and high self-esteem were the keys to success in academics and in life, more recent research indicates that something else is a better predictor of such success.

GOOD GRADES VERSUS DISCIPLINED WORK HABITS

Ask yourself—what is a better predictor of academic and life success?

The answer is self-discipline.

Self-discipline outperforms IQ and self-esteem. How do you get self-discipline? Through developing good habits and persevering.

For a list of habits that your ninth grader should begin to acquire and suggestions for motivating your child to take on these habits, go to Appendix 1, page 62.

THE NINTH-GRADE GUIDE FOR INVOLVED PARENTS

	Good (above average)	Very good (well above average)	Excellent (top 10%)	Outstanding (top 5%)	One of the top few I've encountered (top 1%)
Academic achievement					
Intellectual promise					
Quality of writing					
Creative, original thought					
Productive class discussion					
Respect accorded by faculty					
Disciplined work habits					
Maturity					
Motivation					
Leadership					
Integrity					
Reaction to setbacks					
Concern for others					
Self-confidence					
Initiative, independence					
OVERALL					

© 2011 The Common Application, Inc. Reprinted with permission

GOOD GRADES VERSUS DISCIPLINED WORK HABITS

Some parents hope that with maturity their child will magically acquire these habits in high school. Please don't wait until your child is older to learn these habits. Why? Many parents underestimate the studying time lost when students start studying for their driver's test and friends start driving. By establishing the expectation now that even if there isn't written homework, your child will sit and review, your child will most likely be rated on the far right on the Common Application's teacher evaluation for disciplined work habits.

Reaction to Setbacks

Reaction to setbacks is another category on the teacher evaluation form for the Common Application. Whenever your children have a setback, you naturally react with compassion and concern to mitigate their discomfit. If possible, you will do whatever you can to fix the problem. But this isn't always the best response possible.

In ninth grade, you certainly will have many opportunities to soothe your child, but you must be judicious in what you attempt to fix. If you can steel yourself to let your child have some natural consequences, your child will learn to manage setbacks.

For example, let's say you are at work when you receive a text that your child forgot his project at home. Your instinct may be to call one of the grandparents to drop it off at the front-desk. Then, the receptionist will interrupt the teacher's delivery to thirty students to advise Junior to pick up his project. Don't do it!

REACTION TO SETBACKS

	Good (above average)	Very good (well above average)	Excellent (top 10%)	Outstanding (top 5%)	One of the top few I've encountered (top 1%)
Academic achievement					
Intellectual promise					
Quality of writing					
Creative, original thought					
Productive class discussion					
Respect accorded by faculty					
Disciplined work habits					
Maturity					
Motivation					
Leadership					
Integrity					
Reaction to setbacks					
Concern for others					
Self-confidence					
Initiative, independence					
OVERALL					

© 2011 The Common Application, Inc. Reprinted with permission

THE NINTH-GRADE GUIDE FOR INVOLVED PARENTS

Let your children get the lower grade for lateness. While it may impact their GPA for college transcripts, it will teach them a valuable lesson. Your children will have another estimated thirty projects between now and twelfth grade, and they will have a better chance of remembering them if forced to suffer the embarrassment of not handing in a project. You will hear the moaning—"All that work and I couldn't get an A because I forgot it,"—but you may be providing an opportunity for growth and maturing that other students don't have. If your child's grades dip in ninth and then come back stronger in tenth and eleventh grade, it can be explained in college interviews and essays.

Also, consider it from the perspective of a teacher. When it comes to awards and special opportunities: are we going to recommend a student whose family interrupts class or one who brings in assignments on time? Some parents tell the receptionist to please call between classes, so as not to disrupt. In-between classes, teachers are monitoring the halls, and not near a phone. Also, the receptionist at a large school has too many requests to wait until the end of class.

The same rule applies for forgetting lunch or lunch money, or a permission slip. If some students can't go on a field trip because for two weeks they forgot the slip, then let them have a natural consequence. A healthy respect for deadlines will help your child. If your child doesn't learn in high school to remember

REACTION TO SETBACKS

things, what are you going to do when he or she is in college?

However, if your child has an accident, then by all means drop off a new set of clothes; an unforeseen emergency merits help.

Another common setback is for a student to earn a grade just a few points shy of the desired grade. Usually, a few days before the marking period closes, parents panic that the low grade is going to appear on the report card. Their usual response at this point is:

1. Review all missing assignments and ask if they can now be handed in for credit.

2. Ask for extra credit.

3. Ask to change the grade.

Most teachers will not allow students to turn in missing assignments for credit at the end of the semester.

The purpose of doing assignments is to better learn and apply the material within the context of what is being taught. Cramming to finish assignments just to raise a grade bypasses that essential learning opportunity.

Furthermore, if the grades are online, parents making this request at the end of the marking period have not been adequately managing their child's work. See page 40 about online grade management.

Often, when grades are nearly final, parents will tell their children to ask me for extra credit. I tell them that I always give extra credit but never "instead-of-credit." "Instead-of-credit" means they missed homework, missed projects, and didn't prepare adequately for tests. It masks the underlying problem that led to the lower grade in the first place—a problem that needs to be addressed and corrected.

Look at the example of the Teacher's Evaluation for the Common Application. How will future teachers rate your child in the category "Reaction to setbacks" if your child does nothing to correct the mistakes that led to the low grades in ninth grade? You owe it to your child's future to learn from this mistake, rather than sweep it under the rug.

REACTION TO SETBACKS

Some parents even try to bully teachers to change grades. They tell teachers, "If you don't change this grade, my child won't get into honors/get into the best college/get the best job/have the best life and it will all be your fault."

My child's destiny if you change this grade.

My child's destiny if you don't change this grade.

Do not make this request. It is an illusion born of parental fear and lack of current information about college acceptances.

Most colleges are interested in how students overcome adversity, and having the parents bully the teachers is not one of the preferred responses. If you can problem-solve what the student needs to do to improve, and then he or she does improve, this could become the basis for a powerful "overcoming adversity" essay.

Why do you think colleges are interested in this category?

Many college admission officers have confirmed that colleges are interested in their freshmen retention rate and in the quality of campus life.

They do not want students unaccustomed to setbacks on their campus because it contributes to students' suicides. Cornell University is training professors to help students put academic rigor in proper perspective to offset the six suicides in the past academic year.

Where do you want your child to have his or her first setback? In college, surrounded by students drinking, or at home, surrounded by grounded adults? Help your child to handle academic setbacks by analyzing and correcting the problem in ninth grade; you'll be glad you did.

Initiative and Independence

On the teacher evaluation form for the Common Application, your child will be rated for initiative and independence. How do you strike the right balance between keeping your child safe while taking steps to foster independence?

Universally, ninth-grade teachers want parents to resist the temptation to tell the child, "You are in the big leagues now, let's see how you do and if you can't manage it then we will step in and help." In general, these parents underestimate the amount of previously mentioned sheltering the middle school teachers provided.

While for some students this may work, most students need parents to actively teach them how to break simultaneous projects down into little tasks and complete those tasks long before the deadline. Only a small percentage of adolescents can innately do this.

Students need parents to actively teach them how to manage their time and live a balanced life. The best gift you can give your child is the gift of keeping a planner. You need to motivate your child to:

- ♥ Write down all assignments.
- ♥ Write down all extracurricular activities and appointments.

THE NINTH-GRADE GUIDE FOR INVOLVED PARENTS

	Good (above average)	Very good (well above average)	Excellent (top 10%)	Outstanding (top 5%)	One of the top few I've encountered (top 1%)
Academic achievement					
Intellectual promise					
Quality of writing					
Creative, original thought					
Productive class discussion					
Respect accorded by faculty					
Disciplined work habits					
Maturity					
Motivation					
Leadership					
Integrity					
Reaction to setbacks					
Concern for others					
Self-confidence					
Initiative, independence					
OVERALL					

© 2011 The Common Application, Inc. Reprinted with permission

INITIATIVE AND INDEPENDENCE

- ♥ Break a project into small tasks and assign dates to complete each task.
- ♥ Write down tests and quizzes and assign ten minutes a night to prepare for them in advance of actual test dates.

Today, few students and parents worry about writing down the assignments since they are now available online. However, students then depend on teachers to post it, and on the home computer to be problem-free. This scenario delays independence and creates a future high-maintenance employee who can't independently work.

How do you motivate your child to use a daily planner every day until it becomes a habit? Make it a daily condition for receiving valued electronic time. If your child presents the daily planner with everything recorded, then he or she earns thirty minutes of playing video games or using the computer for social networking, after homework is completed. Parents can check the planner against the assignments posted online.

With independence comes accountability; and students are accountable for work missed while absent. Unlike previous years, the teachers are not going to approach the student about missed work; it is up to the student to approach the teacher at the appropriate time. Actively teaching your child how to do this will create true self-confidence.

THE NINTH-GRADE GUIDE FOR INVOLVED PARENTS

Another important step to being independent is the ability to wake up and appropriately groom. If your child is not up, washed, dressed, and able to grab something to eat by a certain departure time, then he or she cannot take the cell phone or iPod to school. While many parents flinch at denying themselves their safety line to their child, it will help students in the long run. Do it.

Self-Confidence

On the teacher evaluation for the Common Application, your child will also be rated for self-confidence. In my opinion, true self-confidence in the classroom comes from trying one's best academically, from exploring new and appropriate activities just for fun, and from learning how to act appropriately even when one makes a mistake.

Many parents make the mistake of trying to build students' self-esteem by constantly telling children, "You are so smart." Recent research indicates this actually leads to non-performance.

For example, two similar groups of students were given a puzzle to solve. When they had solved it, one group was praised for being smart; the other group was praised for working well together and not giving up. When offered another, more challenging puzzle to do, the group praised for being smart refused and the other group eagerly took on the challenge.

I see this in students who are only interested in doing what is easy for them. It is as if a part of them doesn't want to try something hard and discover that they aren't as smart as their parents tell them—it would be an act of disloyalty toward their parents.

THE NINTH-GRADE GUIDE FOR INVOLVED PARENTS

	Good (above average)	Very good (well above average)	Excellent (top 10%)	Outstanding (top 5%)	One of the top few I've encountered (top 1%)
Academic achievement					
Intellectual promise					
Quality of writing					
Creative, original thought					
Productive class discussion					
Respect accorded by faculty					
Disciplined work habits					
Maturity					
Motivation					
Leadership					
Integrity					
Reaction to setbacks					
Concern for others					
Self-confidence					
Initiative, independence					
OVERALL					

© 2011 The Common Application, Inc. Reprinted with permission.

SELF-CONFIDENCE

In my opinion, being told they are smart leaves students feeling powerless because they did nothing to *be* smart, and therefore they can't do anything to *stay* smart. In my experience, self-confidence comes from persevering and surviving the experience of trying outside the zone of immediate competency. Look to praise your children for actual instances of persevering and working with others, and I believe you will see their true self-confidence increase.

Class Choices

To help your children build self-confidence, let them choose the world language that they want and not the one you want them to take. Ditto for electives.

Also be careful of what you say about learning a language—some parents tell their children that they had four years of a language and can't speak a word of it. They don't mention that they also had other subjects that they don't use and can't retrieve from their memory banks.

Be supportive. With technology, you are going to be impressed with how much access your child will have to using and maintaining the language! If you tell your children about your own shortcomings in an attempt to bolster their confidence, it sometimes leads to a conflict that the children have to choose between surpassing the parent or repeating the parent's experience. Don't do it; it doesn't help.

THE NINTH-GRADE GUIDE FOR INVOLVED PARENTS

Correcting Teacher Errors

You can also help children to build self-confidence by practicing with them how to approach a teacher about missed work and how to inquire politely about an assignment recorded incorrectly. Practice the appropriate tone and timing of the request. This will lead to a more desirable answer and build your children's confidence in their ability to negotiate appropriately with adults.

For example, while I am in the middle of presenting a new idea to the whole class, a student will suddenly raise a hand and announce, "My mother told me to tell you that you forgot to record credit for the homework I missed a few weeks ago when I was on the field trip, but I did show it to you."

To avoid these rude interruptions, show your child how to access a printout of the grades with the date and highlight the item in question to support the student's request. Advise your child to approach the teacher before class starts or at the end of class with the question, "When would be a good time to discuss a missing homework grade with you?"

Secondary teachers record hundreds of grades each week, and we do make mistakes. Recently I accidenttally recorded a grade of "6" out of 100 when the student had actually scored a grade of "86." Ask your ninth graders how and when they would rectify such a mistake. Listen to them and rehearse. This will build self-confidence.

New Year, New Schedule

Another way to build your child's confidence in the beginning of the school year is to help your child to come up with strategies for when to go to the locker, when to go to the bathroom, and how to sort books and binders into morning and afternoon chunks so that the student is not carrying everything all day. Or if your child is on an alternating block schedule, label everything "A" days and "B" days or "odd" days and "even" days—whatever code the school uses. See Appendix 4, page 80 and Appendix 5, page 82.

A firm grasp of time is also important. Future employers will demand that employees be aware of time and show up on time. Our local hospital uses sensors on their ID badges to track their employees' time.

Is your child's school building old? If so, the clocks may all be analog and many students today never quite know what time it is because they can't read analog clocks after half past and they are forbidden from checking their cell phones for the correct time in school. Yet with a bell schedule, students are expected to be more aware of time, and those who do exude more self-confidence.

THE NINTH-GRADE GUIDE FOR INVOLVED PARENTS

To build confidence, either encourage your student to wear a digital watch or use the school's bell schedule to practice at home how many minutes are left in the class, based on the analog clock. (This may seem silly, but after I tell parents this, they frequently report back to me that they were amazed that their child couldn't decipher how many minutes were left in the class and felt constantly helpless around these issues of time.)

Ninth graders have a warped sense of time. They fear going to their locker or putting their papers in the correct folder will take more time than it actually does. Encourage them to actually time how long it takes. This will build confidence that they can do things quickly. Also, point out the number of minutes it actually takes may be distorted if they are also trying to text and listen to their iPods simultaneously. Remind them to focus on the task at hand.

Speaking of numbers, some students start the school year poorly because the first pages of their textbooks are in Roman numerals and they never quite know what these are. Help them with this and they will be more confident from day one of the new school year.

Online Grades

Some parents mistakenly believe they can build their child's self-confidence by relying on the child to learn how to use the online grading program. Invariably,

SELF-CONFIDENCE

parents who boast that their computer-savvy children show them their grades—and that they never have to check grades themselves—regret that decision when they realize that their children are selectively sharing information.

Students need to know that that their parents will look beyond the summary page of grade averages and be able to click on the individual subject to read the comments about classroom behavior and other information that teachers are sharing vis-à-vis the online grading program.

It makes them accountable, makes them feel safe and secure, and prevents them from making themselves crazy with fear about what will happen when their parents ultimately discover the truth.

Does your school have two kinds of log-in systems for the online grading program, one for students and one for parents? If so, it is best to keep them separate. Always use your own log-in. This allows teachers to confirm that <u>parents</u> have read their comments. If your child uses your log-in, we may believe it's you, and you may never receive important information.

Become familiar with the teachers' web pages with links. Some teachers upload their grading rubrics and their handouts to their teacher page. Review the website with your child. If two students misplace the worksheet for homework, and one goes to the website and prints out a copy while the other doesn't, who do you think will feel more self-confident entering class the next day?

Sometimes online grades undermine students' self-confidence because parents don't wait to discuss any issues with the student. Instead, they immediately e-mail the teacher. Parents should fight this temptation and wait until they can discuss face-to-face any concerns with the child. It gives the child practice discussing disappointing news, and, once past the unpleasantness, the child will realize that he or she survived and moved on. This instills self-confidence.

Parents used to receive updated progress reports from quarterly reports and interim reports. Now parents can access grades a few times a day if they so desire. (In my experience, some do!) The problem is that sometimes parents have so much information that they focus on grades rather than learning. I once had a student who peppered me with the expressions, "How many points is this worth? Is this for a grade?" When we had a one-on-one talk, he told me that his parents only cared about his grades, and that any ungraded activity that would help him to learn was not valued.

He and his parents never discussed what he was learning, or what book he was reading. As the other students learned to speak Spanish, to make connections to cognates in English, and to bring in

SELF-CONFIDENCE

examples of songs and words in Spanish that they found just for fun, their confidence grew. Meanwhile this student appeared to be more anxious and less confident.

When parents engage their children in dialogues about what they are learning—when they ask their child to explain a concept or why something was important historically and not just engage their child in status reports on grades—students believe that what they are learning is important. Therefore, *they* are important—it builds self-confidence.

New Friends

You and your child may be anxious over the summer about the next year's schedule. Most students are anxious about having a friend at the same lunch, and having friends from middle school in their classes.

Their self-confidence slips when they feel that none of their friends are in their classes. To offset this, parents can help their children to feel confident about making new friends by helping them to recognize when they are already good at making new acquaintances.

Point out times when they make new friends quickly: when they play with students on a team and some aren't from their school, or when they join a group at your place of worship, or while they are visiting a cousin and playing nicely with his or her friends. This

THE NINTH-GRADE GUIDE FOR INVOLVED PARENTS

will help your child to feel confident about making new friends. Remind your children that their current school friends may take the same bus home, or that they might walk home together. Encourage your child to sign up for the same after-school activity as their friends. Usually, there are many activities that do not involve sports or academics.

Also, remind them of the old Girl Scouts song:

Make new friends,

but keep the old;

one is silver and the other gold.

Respect Accorded by Faculty

When students apply to colleges, they need to ask a faculty member to write a teacher evaluation that includes a rating for the amount of respect the other faculty members have for them.

Few faculty members respect students who respond poorly to corrections, lie to avoid a consequence, or treat other students badly.

Respond Poorly to Corrections

When I grew up in the 50s, the social contract was that all adults had the obligation to correct all children. Children never took it personally, nor did they challenge the adults' authority. Today, some families take teachers' corrections personally. These families need to depersonalize the corrections.

Adolescents will try out new behaviors, and adults—including teachers—*are obliged* to respond to them. How the adolescent responds to the correction will partially determine the amount of respect accorded by the faculty.

How do you train ninth graders to respond gracefully to a correction? Use the A–C–T (Adult-Child-Teenager) system to redirect the child's response. This system depersonalizes their behavior and helps adults to remember to depersonalize their reactions.

THE NINTH-GRADE GUIDE FOR INVOLVED PARENTS

	Good (above average)	Very good (well above average)	Excellent (top 10%)	Outstanding (top 5%)	One of the top few I've encountered (top 1%)
Academic achievement					
Intellectual promise					
Quality of writing					
Creative, original thought					
Productive class discussion					
Respect accorded by faculty					
Disciplined work habits					
Maturity					
Motivation					
Leadership					
Integrity					
Reaction to setbacks					
Concern for others					
Self-confidence					
Initiative, independence					
OVERALL					

© 2011 The Common Application, Inc. Reprinted with permission.

RESPECT ACCORDED BY FACULTY

A-C-T

Little Children respond to corrections with four tactics:

TACTIC

DENY
"No, I'm not…"
"That's not true."

DIVERT
"So and so is…"
"But yesterday X did…"
"Everyone…"

CHALLENGE
"Why do you always…"
"No other parent…"

THREATEN
"Dad says…"
"I'm never gonna visit you…"
"I'm telling Protective Services…"

Mature Teenagers take ownership of mistakes.
Mature Teenagers do not need to have the last word.
Mature Teenagers process a conflict internally.
Mature Teenagers respond to corrections with:

RESPONSE

APOLOGIZE
"Sorry."

"My bad."

REFLECT
"That was a mistake. I probably hurt _____ by doing that. I can fix this by _____. I won't make that mistake again."

GROW
"Thanks for caring enough about me to help me improve. This will help me to be a better person and fulfill my destiny."

POST IT:	At home, put a copy of the chart on the refrigerator or on a little card, wherever you will see it to remind you how to train your child.
EXPLAIN IT:	During a neutral time, explain to your children that a little child and an emerging mature teen reside in each of them. Tell them at some point they may act as a little child, and that you are going to walk over to the poster and point out which tactic they are using and invite them to take a step on the path of becoming a mature teenager. Some days they will, and some days they won't be able to.
UNDERSTAND IT:	As the adult, don't take their outburst personally. Understand it is just where they are on their own path to maturity. If they persist, tell them that they need to take that dialogue inside in order to grow. Frequently, when I use the chart in class, if the student prolongs the episode, other students will chime in, urging the student to stop acting like a little kid or a baby.

Now, let's practice managing the discussion when a parent confronts a child with an unpleasant truth and the child responds with one of the four tactics.

RESPECT ACCORDED BY FACULTY

∞∞∞

SITUATION: You check online, or the teacher calls you and you discover that your child is missing multiple assignments.

DENY   "No, I'm not!"

"That's not true!" "I did them in study hall."

SOLUTION
"OK, I understand that as a parent to a ninth grader, we will run through four responses until we resolve this. We are right on target with the first one, denial. (Take out the little card if necessary.) It feels like the little child part of you is reacting by denying, and to your age group, it probably feels like you haven't missed that many assignments but in reality you have and we need to figure out why. If you can't get past denying, then we need to come back to this in a little while and until we do, X privilege is off-limits."

DIVERT   "The teacher loses my work."

"The teacher doesn't like me."

SOLUTION
"OK, the little child part of you is reacting by diverting, but I need you to not take the role of the victim. You're not a victim, nor will pretending it's someone else's fault help you to figure out how to get the work done. I need you to take a step towards being a

mature teenager and take responsibility; can you do that for me today? No, well, perhaps tomorrow will be better—I know you will get there. We need to come back to this in a little while and until we do, X privilege is off-limits."

CHALLENGE "Why don't you trust me?

"All of the other parents know that this teacher is a problem but you."

SOLUTION
"OK, the little child part of you is reacting by challenging me, but in order for you to learn how to balance all of these different assignments, we need to focus on what you can do. You are not to challenge my job as your parent and the adult in charge. We need to get you to the point where we can problem-solve why your work isn't being completed and handed in. A good start would be for you to apologize, but we must address this issue. If you can't be part of a dialogue about this then we need to take away X privilege and we'll start again later. Can you do that for me today? No, well, perhaps tomorrow will be better—I have seen many glimpses of you being very mature for your age and I know I will see them again."

THREATEN "I'm gonna go live with Dad."

RESPECT ACCORDED BY FACULTY

"I'm gonna report you as being a bad parent."

SOLUTION
"OK, the little child part of you is reacting by threatening me, and it sounds like you are willing to turn on me rather than deal with this problem. You must be really afraid that you will have to make some scary changes in order to get your work done—so scary that you will threaten your best source of help. I suspect you will have to give up X in order to get your assignments all done—is that what concerns you?"

∞∞∞

After all of this repetition, you probably have the solution part memorized. Great! Now memorize the words: *deny, divert, challenge, and threaten*. Begin to closely observe others; practice labeling reactions in your mind and soon the correct response will fall out of your mouth naturally!

When you help your children to identify their own tactics, they can begin to act as mature teenagers when they are responding to corrections by teachers. This will go a long way in earning their teachers' respect.

Lies

If you want your child to stand out among other students, encourage your child to tell the truth and accept the consequences of a mistake graciously. Model this behavior. Based on my observations of ninth graders, the new moral code is to lie and never admit a mistake; as I saw on one boy's tee shirt, "If you don't get caught, it isn't wrong!"

For example, the students in French class watch *Au Revoir, Les Enfants*, a movie about students during the Holocaust. There is a scene where the priest confiscates hidden food and asks the group of boys to identify which item belongs to which student. Each student admits to owning the individual item.

When we first started showing this movie years ago, this scene garnered no response from students; they were more concerned about the Jewish students rounded up for the concentration camps. However, today's students spend an inordinate amount of time marveling that anyone would admit to having a forbidden item. They don't understand why a student would admit to a mistake that will certainly extract a consequence.

Here is a list of lies and statements to avoid responsibility that diminish a teacher's respect for a student:

- ♥ "I didn't know there was homework." (Did you check online, write it down, or call a friend?)

- ♥ "I didn't know how to do it." (Did you ask questions in class when it was assigned? Did you

RESPECT ACCORDED BY FACULTY

start it so late you couldn't call anyone? Did you check online on the teacher's page for help?)

- ♥ "I got a low grade on the project because the teacher doesn't like me." (Did the teacher hand back a rubric? What did it say?)

- ♥ "I had a big project in another class, so I didn't do your homework." (Did you leave the work until the last minute? Why didn't you start the other project sooner?)

- ♥ "I didn't know we were having a test today." (Why not? It has been posted online, and on the board for a week, and the other students all know.)

- ♥ "The homework is in my locker. Can I show you after lunch?" (The student is going to do it at lunch. I've had a student go to her locker, and stay around the corner and write it out, pretending it had been in the locker all along.)

Help your children to accept consequences and not lie to teachers; they will be ranked well in respect accorded by faculty, providing they also show concern for others, which we'll discuss next.

Concern for Others

At some point in your child's adolescence, you may hear from a teacher, principal, professional school counselor, or parent of another child that your child was mean to another person.

Your first reaction may very well be, "No one knows my child like I do, and my child wouldn't ever do such a thing."

It is true that parents know their child best within the context of their home and the activities they orchestrate for their child. It is also true that while they were experts on "Child Jamie," they may need time to understand their new "Adolescent Jamie."

According to David Walsh in *Why Do They Act That Way*, new brain growth creates "Adolescent Jamie" who will act out of character. Furthermore, "Adolescent Jamie," in the classroom with thirty other students, may be playing to an audience that the parents don't know.

It is hard for parents to learn some unpleasant information about their child. However, it is even harder down the road when they believe that their child has the perfect transcript for a certain college and don't realize that the teacher doing the evaluation has to rate the child unfavorably in the category "Concern for others."

CONCERN FOR OTHERS

	Good (above average)	Very good (well above average)	Excellent (top 10%)	Outstanding (top 5%)	One of the top few I've encountered (top 1%)
Academic achievement					
Intellectual promise					
Quality of writing					
Creative, original thought					
Productive class discussion					
Respect accorded by faculty					
Disciplined work habits					
Maturity					
Motivation					
Leadership					
Integrity					
Reaction to setbacks					
Concern for others					
Self-confidence					
Initiative, independence					
OVERALL					

© 2011 The Common Application, Inc. Reprinted with permission

THE NINTH-GRADE GUIDE FOR INVOLVED PARENTS

When children receive a poor evaluation, oftentimes the parents are to blame: they refused to hear from teachers about the way their child treats others and missed the opportunity to correct the problem.

This is your chance. If the inappropriate behavior is addressed now, it will be just a temporary phase. Corrected, it won't derail a child's future.

"Our little girl is so sweet."

"So sweet, she would never hurt a fly!"

CONCERN FOR OTHERS

Or would she?

It can be a challenge to teach students to develop concern for others. Today's students are so often plugged in with tweeting, Facebooking, and texting that other people seem to be melding into chronic "white-noise" background.

To offset students' indifference to others, many schools now require "community service" hours as a requirement for graduation. But this institutionalized compassion also compartmentalizes doing the right thing for X hours outside of normal day-to-day life.

Here are some of the behaviors that students should practice to develop consideration for others:

- ♥ Helping other students to understand a concept, not just giving them the correct answer.

- ♥ Saying "hi" and giving high-fives to the special education students in the halls.

THE NINTH-GRADE GUIDE FOR INVOLVED PARENTS

- ♥ Helping a student with dropped items in the classroom or hall.

- ♥ Seeking out the teacher when no other student is around and reporting other students' bullying behavior so that the teacher can catch it.

- ♥ Offering to distribute papers or collect items the teacher handed out in class.

- ♥ Picking up after themselves, not leaving papers or trash on the floor.

- ♥ Offering to escort someone to the nurse who isn't feeling well.

Discuss these items with your ninth graders. Ask your child to identify behaviors they have seen in the hall that were kind and respectful to other students. Remind your children that doing considerate acts only for extra points or other rewards negates doing the right thing.

Conclusion

My favorite Brazilian legend is the "Pai Coruja." This "father owl" was enamored with his three new babies. He begged the predator, the hawk, to leave his babies alone. The hawk agreed and asked for a description so that he wouldn't eat this owl's babies. The *pai coruja* described them as beautiful, strong, smart, and bright-eyed. A few days later, the babies were missing and a sparrow told the *pai coruja* that the hawk had eaten them! When the *pai coruja* confronted the hawk, he exclaimed, "I didn't know they were yours because they were so ugly, weak, and stupid!"

I love this legend because it warns parents that only by abandoning their illusions about their children can they truly protect them.

My sister, the mother of four, never valued this story whenever I told it. She wondered, "What was wrong with the hawk that it couldn't tell how special the babies were?" Now the story clicks for her because she is the grandmother of seven. She struggles with loyalty to protecting her own children's illusions about their children and loyalty to getting the right help for her grandchildren.

Misguided parents need concerned teachers, friends, neighbors, and family members to support them and their children on the path of a strong work ethic and on the path where actions and decisions do have consequences. This path will positively impact the child's teacher evaluation for the Common Application and it will help the children to be responsible adults and employees.

It isn't easy when other parents continue on the path of enabling, but you need to make parenting decisions based on your child's long-term future: graduating college and being successful in a job, just not getting into the desired college.

Be strong. Resist succumbing to illusions because of your fear and because of what other parents are doing. Do the right thing. Our country and our economy need strong parents now more than ever.

Keep fighting the good fight!

                                        Ellen Shrager

THE NINTH-GRADE GUIDE FOR INVOLVED PARENTS

APPENDICES

Appendix 1—Habits Students Need

We baby boomers owe an apology to our children for giving everyone a trophy for just showing up: many students expect good grades in exchange for "**no-hassle seat time.**"

If your child's performance doesn't reflect his or her true ability, there may be a disconnect between your definition of studying and your child's definition of studying. For example, a student asked me, "Why is my grade so low, I studied, I was prepared!" To my baby-boomer ears, that means the student reviewed notes every night since the last test, spent an hour the prior weekend reviewing, and probably another half hour the evening before and got a good night's sleep before eating a breakfast with a protein that morning. What would it mean to you?

To the student, it meant he didn't miss any classes, crammed during the half-hour study hall opposite lunch that day, and asked his friends during lunch about the test because they had already taken it.

In order to reach a meeting of the minds, use the Student Performance Charts on the next few pages. You want to determine the following:

1. Your child's homework profile.
2. Your child's study habits.
3. Your child's attitudes towards grades.

Ask yourself which box number represents your child's usual effort? Keep it to yourself. Then, in a neutral tone, ask your child which box number represents his or her current approach—amazingly, students are honest. Then, show them what they need to be doing to do better. Create a dialogue about what needs to change in order for all to be happy.

APPENDIX 1—HABITS STUDENTS NEED

STUDENT PERFORMANCE CHARTS

WRITTEN HOMEWORK

1	2	3
We copy from others and hand in their work for our points.	We choose not to do our homework and are polite when we tell the teacher we don't have it.	We just quickly do the written homework—unless something unusual comes up.
4	**5**	**6**
We do all of our homework to the best of our ability. We do every extra credit assignment we can.	We do all of our written homework and practice concepts and definitions.	We do all of our homework, including reviewing chapters. We look for connections in other classes.

NON-WRITTEN HOMEWORK

1	2	3
We are relieved that the home-work is "just" learning the material—we don't have to do anything.	We learn only what we hear in class. We do not memorize outside of class.	We put off memorizing. We cram before a quiz. We learn the easy stuff, but not the difficult part.
4	**5**	**6**
We learn new info every night with flash cards, reading, writing, making a tape or song—whatever it takes.	We review all of the material even on the nights no homework is assigned.	We review the summary pages for each chapter and the class notes sections in our notebooks.

APPENDIX 1—HABITS STUDENTS NEED

STUDY HABITS

1	2	3
We don't worry about studying; we sit next to the right person, make cheat sheets, leave open books on the floor, and write on our hands and desks.	We choose to do other things than study. We don't care how we do on the test.	We study the night before a test and sometimes during lunch, but we are so overwhelmed by all we've forgotten, we get hysterical and/or discouraged.
4	**5**	**6**
Our parents, our teacher, and we ourselves know that we have been preparing since the first day that this material was presented. We tell ourselves we have done our best but we still worry.	We start studying for major tests the previous weekend.	We have been reviewing and studying continuously and are eager to prove what we know.

THE NINTH-GRADE GUIDE FOR INVOLVED PARENTS

ATTITUDES TOWARDS GRADES

1	2	3
When caught cheating, we loudly protest it's no big deal to cheat. We prove that the teacher erroneously gave another student the points for the wrong answer and we want that credit also!	We accept our decision to not study and accept the grade we earn. We tell ourselves that we could do better, but we are not interested in using our talents for schoolwork.	We are surprised when we don't do well on tests because we did do some work. We need good grades to keep our parents happy. We don't make corrections and learn from our mistakes—we just want the grade.
4	**5**	**6**
Sometimes we sigh that if we had other people's ability with our work ethic, we would be on top. Our grades don't reflect all the work we do. We feel good about doing our best. We make corrections and learn from our mistakes because learning is cumulative.	Our grades reflect our hard work and we are pleased. We are curious about our mistakes. We aren't just interested in the grade.	We can usually predict what we didn't know, and as soon as the test is over, we look up the answers we missed. We make corrections and ask "why?"

APPENDIX 1—HABITS STUDENTS NEED

After discussing the Student Performance Charts, you may realize that your child needs better habits.

Look at the habits on the following pages. Are there any that your child needs to take on? Please, please, please, don't try all of them at once. But start with the one that would change your child's life the most and stick with it until it becomes a habit.

Then—and only then—move on to the next.

I did the homework. I had it earlier. Now where is it????

KNOW WHAT TO DO
AT THE BEGINNING OF CLASS

1. Is my homework out?
2. Is my binder/folder/book for this class out?
3. Do I have my pencil and pen? Is my pencil sharpened?
4. Do I have my assignment book ready?
5. What is the pre-class/bell ringer activity?

THE NINTH-GRADE GUIDE FOR INVOLVED PARENTS

KNOW WHAT TO DO AT THE END OF CLASS

1. Is my homework in the homework folder?
2. Did I copy down the assignment?
3. Did I hand in everything for this class?
4. Did I punch holes/put papers in the right binder/folder?
5. Is my binder/folder/book in my bag?
6. Are my pencils/hole punch/sharpener in their right places?
7. Did I leave anything under my desk or on my chair?
8. Do I have trash to toss?
9. Do I know where I am going next?

AFTERNOON/EVENING HABITS

1. At my locker, which books/binders/folders/gym stuff do I need?
2. Did I plan my relaxation and homework time?
3. Did I start and finish my homework using a timer?
4. If I don't have written work for a class, did I study my notes?
5. Did I put my homework/books/binders/folders in my book bag?
6. Did I work fifteen minutes on projects not due tomorrow?
7. Did I get papers signed for school and returned
8. Did I replace my tissues and pencils and any other supplies?
9. Do I have my clothes laid out for tomorrow?

APPENDIX 1—HABITS STUDENTS NEED

10. Did I put dirty gym clothes in the laundry and pack new ones?
11. Do I have my sports equipment/after-school-activity supplies?
12. Do I have my band instrument/books and supplies for the classes that don't meet every day?
13. Do I have my bus badge/student ID/lunch/lunch money?
14. Is my alarm set? Am I going to bed at a reasonable time?
15. Did I plan for breakfast?

HOW TO DO PROJECTS

1. List tasks to do (e.g., project components.)
2. List supplies needed/when to get them, including:
   a. back-up ink/paper/file storage/Internet;
   b. computer programs compatible with school.
3. Estimate amount of time for each task.
4. On calendar, with adult, assign daily tasks.
5. Follow calendar and check off tasks.
6. Pack it! Bring it to school! Bring it to class!

All of these lists are designed to fit on laminated business cards, using a smaller font. Utilizing the front and back, they fit on three separate cards I call "habit cards." Here is how I use them in class with my students.

THE NINTH-GRADE GUIDE FOR INVOLVED PARENTS

Before I show the students the first card, I tell them that it is my personal belief that right before they are born, they get to choose a line to stand in. Some babies stand in the musically talented line, some stand in the athletically talented line, some stand in the organized line, and I think I missed those lines because I was in the chocolate line.

I ask students to think about what line they were in and they tell me what talents they have. I do this because I don't want them to feel bad if they weren't born organized. With effort, they can learn how to be organized. At the same time, people born organized may not have their talents.

I then ask students to discuss what they think about as they enter the classroom. I explain that people born organized think about the list on the first card; sometimes it is a revelation to students not born organized that others automatically have these habits.

I ask them to look at the list on the first card and tell me which habits they already have and which habits they need to develop. I ask the students which habit would change their life the most, and that is the one they start with. I urge them to take on one habit at a time until the habit is automatic and then try another until they've worked through all three cards. Many report back that this is all they needed and it is working for them.

APPENDIX 1—HABITS STUDENTS NEED

Sometimes, however, parents tell me they have tried everything to organize their child. Perhaps they have even written out the habits that their child needs. Yet the child has no inner voice that guides him or her to implement the organization. We need to give this child that inner dialogue. Here is how I help such students

I tell students that my mother and I used to talk about how we were like the trees that are cut to reveal a ring for every year of their life. My mother had eighty-two rings but sometimes she felt that she was on her sixteenth ring and sometimes she felt that she was on her fourth ring. I feel the same way and can jump to different rings during the course of a day.

I tell students that the essence of adolescence is to also jump frequently to different rings. They may hover on the little child rings, jump to a very mature ring beyond their current age, then jump to their age ring, and start all over again.

I ask them to think about who they will be fifteen years from now. If they envision themselves being a professional athlete, I reserve my speech about the odds of that happening and having a plan B for some other time. I ask them to give a name to that vision of themselves. One student told me she was going to be an artist, and she named the older version of herself "Le Artiste."

THE NINTH-GRADE GUIDE FOR INVOLVED PARENTS

If the students are unsure of what the future holds, I ask them to tell me what kind of car they will be driving or where they might be living. One such student called himself "Corvy" because he wants to own a corvette. For my purpose, I'll use "Famous Writer."

Then I ask them for a nickname from when they were little to represent when they are on one of the little child rings. Frequently they use a name that their grandparents call them. For my purposes, I'll use "Little Ellie."

I then point out to students that when they are on a little kid ring, they never ever want to stop playing video games, shut off the TV, or stop any pleasurable activity. The thought of stopping feels like the little child will die and never have fun again.

I urge them to talk to that little one like this: *"OK, Little Ellie, I know you don't want me to start studying, but it will only be for ten minutes. I will set the timer and when it dings, I will be right back. I need to do this so twelve-year-old Ellen can get good habits, and Famous Writer can get a good job, and have lots of time to indulge you. Famous Writer will thank twelve-year-old Ellen for learning how to do this now."*

After using a timer to switch back and forth between pleasurable activities and school work for ten minutes at a time (or else their age plus two minutes),

APPENDIX 1—HABITS STUDENTS NEED

students report back to me that this gets them over their inertia. Many eventually decide to just do the work for an hour straight so that they can then have more prolonged fun time.

What if none of this works and the child is still stuck and can't do anything? If I knew the one magic dialogue that would solve the problem of the student who does nothing, I would be writing this from my private island in Brazil. Instead, there is snow around the bird feeder as I look out my window, write these words, and prepare tomorrow's lesson plans.

Sometimes there is an untransmitted message that the student has internalized even though no person has transmitted that message—it is part of the student's paradigm.

For example, I am the fourth child; I always believed if I had been a boy, we wouldn't have had my baby brother—that being a girl was a disappointment to my parents. Only beside my father's deathbed did I discover that the last three children were unplanned. To make sense of our chaotic, overcrowded house, I concocted a story that blamed myself.

Natalie Rathvon's *Unmotivated Child* breaks down the categories of untransmitted messages that can lead to a child who does nothing. In a nutshell, concocted messages may be about:

THE NINTH-GRADE GUIDE FOR INVOLVED PARENTS

- Children fear surpassing a parent's academic achievement or choose to quit rather than compete with an extraordinarily gifted family member.

- Most adolescent children question their birthright and move on, but some children don't move on. They develop some kind of complicated adoption/divorce/half-siblings wrinkle that they can't get past.

- Children believe that work is dreadful—they don't want to be successful like X, who is never home for the family.

If any of these may explain your child's lack of focus and organization, I would urge you to try Rathvon's book and see where it takes you. Usually this isn't something you can do overnight, but, gradually, with professional help, the problem can be turned around. Remember, you don't intentionally transmit the twisted messages your children create, but you can intentionally get them the help they need to rework the messages so that they stop doing nothing.

APPENDIX 2—THE MYTH OF THE HEAVY PACKBACK

Appendix 2—The Myth Of The Heavy Backpack

The media wrongly blames schools for heavy backpacks! Students lug them when they are anxious about being late to class or forgetting something.

SOLUTION:

1) To help them with their anxiety about being late, you can meet them after school and walk out their schedule, analyzing the best time to go to their locker and timing actual trips to the locker. They are amazed that there is time if they focus and hustle! If you can't arrange your schedule to do this you can ask the school counselor to find someone to do it with your student.

THE NINTH-GRADE GUIDE FOR INVOLVED PARENTS

2) Some parents insist on one heavy binder so their students won't forget anything. I suggest you give students two cloth bags, an AM and a PM, which slip into their school bags or else hang in their lockers. Each bag is labeled with what books/supplies should be in it. They switch to an AM and a PM binder. In the morning, they divide items brought from home into the two bags. In the afternoon, before leaving for home, they take what they need from each bag and leave the bags in their lockers. It works!

3) If on a block schedule, label the bags and binders according to the school system, i.e., "A" and "B" days or "odd" and "even" days.

4) Parents should go through the book bags with their children nightly if they are unorganized, otherwise weekly.

Appendix 3—Avoiding Dress Code Violations

Some adolescents choose to act out by violating the dress code. Often the trouble starts on the way to school, after they've passed their parents' inspection. Girls roll up their shorts, tie rubber bands around the shirts, and take off their little sweaters to reveal their spaghetti straps. Boys stash their belts in their backpacks. When parents receive phone call about dress code violations, they need to ask the teacher to describe what the child is wearing before they react to the situation.

From my perspective, the dress code protects the girls from having to dress in sexually provocative clothes in order to fit in. When the dress code is eroded because parents and students loudly protest that it is unfair, or because they insist that male teachers enforcing the dress code are sexual predators for noticing, it is a hollow victory, because we are abandoning our responsibility to keep the children emotionally safe.

Boys are distracted from paying attention by the barrage of flesh in the classrooms, and girls feel they must wear less and less to fit in. Boys may interpret a girl's clothing as a billboard that she is sexually inviting, and then get incensed that their attention, comments, and touches are unwelcomed in the staircase.

Please gather the parents of your daughters' friends together and make a pact to buy school clothes that protect your daughters from unwanted sexual advances.

While we are at it, why do parents allow their growing children to wear flip-flops to school rather than sturdy shoes? Wearing them all the time can lead to foot trouble. Just google "flip flops and foot damage" and then decide if you really want to spend time at the doctor's office with your child's joint pain, shin splints, and twisted ankles.

More than one accident has occurred at my school because students have accidentally stepped on the back of someone's flip-flop in a crowded stairway. This sends the student flying, banging the mouth, and cracking the teeth.

Also, students who wear flip-flops to class tend to remove them in class, and their feet get dirty quickly.

Many employers consider flip-flops unsafe and ban them from the workplace. Help your child to learn that there are boundaries regarding dress codes at work and that using common sense for school outfits is good practice for later.

Appendix 4—Making the Transition to a New Building

Parents can help their children to smoothly transition to a new school building by attending the school tours and the Open House for parents. Follow these steps:

1. Inquire if a bottle of painkiller can be kept at the health suite for your student if you send in a doctor's note for the occasional cramps or headaches. Inform the nurse of any medical issues.

2. Determine the school protocol for letting teachers know if there is something going on. In some schools, you contact the professional school counselor, and some schools you contact the lead teacher.

3. Learn how to use the online grading system, if there is one.

4. Learn where to pick up your child if the nurse is sending him or her home sick.

5. Ditto for the procedures for early dismissal if your child has a dental appointment, for example.

6. Read the handouts that the teachers send home the first day about class rules. If your child is going to lose points for not having a

pencil, send in a good supply to be kept in the locker.

7. Read the student handbook carefully.

8. Procure the room map of the new building and highlight the rooms where your child has classes. Review with your child the locations of the bathrooms, office, locker, nurse, and professional school counselor.

9. Find out the nuances of the late-activity buses if your school has them. Some routes may be condensed; make sure your child knows where the bus stops. If the route is different from the usual bus, make sure your child knows how to get home from there even if it is dusk.

10. Inquire about the e-mail listserv at the school and join it. Spend time on the school's website; there is usually valuable information.

11. Find out if there are opportunities for your child to receive extra tutoring during the school day or after school, and how students go about making up missed quizzes and tests

APPENDIX 5—SUMMER SUGGESTIONS

While summer is definitely the time to relax and renew, it is also the time to begin to equip your children with the "soft skills" that they also need to be successful in school.

1. If your goal is for your children to attend college, then each summer they should be adding skills that will help them to thrive. Consider making this summer be the time that they become responsible for their own laundry or responsible for preparing one meal a week for the family.

2. Look for opportunities for your children to negotiate with other adults (e.g., in restaurants, in stores, at the library, or at the doctor's office). This will help them to be comfortable speaking to teachers and administrators about misunderstandings or problems.

3. If your children play fall sports, use the summer to schedule the check-up with the doctor and fill out the necessary forms for your children play sports, well before the deadline. Model for them how to avoid leaving things until the last minute, an important skill for completing school projects.

THE NINTH-GRADE GUIDE FOR INVOLVED PARENTS

4. Adjust your children's "plugged-in time" to summer hours, but still have limits. Unlimited video games and or social networking can be addictive and will make it very hard for them to adjust to a schedule in September.

5. Give children limits on their texting; otherwise, they will feel comfortable texting and driving, texting in class, texting and walking into traffic, texting and working. A recent news story illustrated that the passengers in a car all braced themselves for an accident and were unhurt, except for the passenger hunched over her phone texting; her phone damaged her vision.

6. Communicate with the parents of your children's friends and form a united front about summer boundaries.

7. On the first day of school, spend time going through the information that each teacher gives out for each class. Even if there is no written homework, start the habit of spending time reviewing the school day, class by class, with your student.

8. Check to see if your school has assigned summer reading to students; if so, make sure it is completed. Consider reading the book and discussing it together.

Appendix 6—Institutions Accepting the Common Application

Following is the list of institutions currently using the Common Application for the 2012-2013 academic year. (Please note that the list is copyrighted © 2011 The Common Application, Inc. Reprinted with permission.)

You might want to visit their website *www.commonapp.org* for an updated list of institutions and for the other forms students need to submit.

There are many fine colleges on this list. There are also many fine colleges not on this list. If you have a particular college in mind for your child, and the college is not listed below, you most likely can view the required application forms online. Pay particular attention to:

- the form for the teacher recommendation
- the form for extracurricular activities
- the form for essay topics
- the form for explaining a low grade

While scanning this list, you will notice that some schools have an asterisk. This indicates that the school requires an extra page or pages in addition to the Common Application

1. Adelphi University

THE NINTH-GRADE GUIDE FOR INVOLVED PARENTS

2. Agnes Scott College
3. Alaska Pacific University
4. Albany College of Pharmacy and Health Sciences
5. Albion College
6. Albright College
7. Alfred University
8. Allegheny College
9. American University
10. Amherst College
11. Arcadia University
12. Assumption College
13. Augsburg College
14. Augustana College (Illinois)
15. Augustana College (South Dakota)
16. Austin College
17. Babson College
18. Baldwin-Wallace College
19. Bard College
20. Barnard College
21. Bates College
22. Belmont University
23. Beloit College
24. Bennington College
25. Bentley University
26. Berry College
27. Birmingham Southern College
28. Boston College
29. Boston University
30. Bowdoin College
31. Bradley University
32. Brandeis University
33. Brown University
34. Bryant University

Appendix 6—Institutions Accepting the Common Application

35. Bryn Mawr College
36. Bucknell University
37. Burlington College
38. Butler University
39. Caldwell College
40. California Institute of Technology (Caltech)
41. California Lutheran University
42. Canisius College
43. Carleton College
44. Carnegie Mellon University
45. Carroll College (Montana)
46. Carroll University
47. Case Western Reserve University
48. Castleton State College
49. Cazenovia College
50. Cedar Crest College
51. Centenary College (Louisiana)
52. Centenary College (NJ)
53. Centre College
54. Champlain College
55. Chapman University
56. Chatham University
57. Christian Brothers University
58. Christopher Newport University
59. Claremont McKenna College
60. Clarkson University
61. Clark University
62. Coe College
63. Colby College
64. Colby-Sawyer College
65. Colgate University
66. College of Mount Saint Vincent
67. College of the Atlantic

THE NINTH-GRADE GUIDE FOR INVOLVED PARENTS

68. College of the Holy Cross
69. College of William & Mary
70. College of Wooster
71. Colorado College
72. Colorado State University
73. Columbia College Chicago
74. Columbia University
75. Concordia College
76. Concordia University
77. Connecticut College
78. Converse College
79. Cornell College
80. Cornell University
81. Creighton University
82. Curry College
83. Daemen College
84. Dartmouth College
85. Davidson College
86. Denison University
87. DePaul University
88. DePauw University
89. DeSales University
90. Dickinson College
91. Dominican University of California
92. Dowling College
93. Drake University
94. Drew University
95. Drexel University
96. Drury University
97. Duke University
98. Earlham College
99. Eastern Connecticut State University
100. Eckerd College

Appendix 6—Institutions Accepting the Common Application

101. Elizabethtown College
102. Elmira College
103. Emerson College
104. Emmanuel College
105. Emory University
106. Fairfield University
107. Fisk University
108. Flagler College
109. Florida Institute of Technology
110. Florida Southern College
111. Fontbonne University
112. Fordham University
113. Franklin and Marshall College
114. Franklin College Switzerland
115. Franklin Pierce University
116. Franklin W. Olin College of Engineering
117. Furman University
118. Gannon University
119. Gettysburg College
120. Gonzaga University
121. Goshen College
122. Goucher College
123. Green Mountain College
124. Grinnell College
125. Guilford College
126. Gustavus Adolphus College
127. Hamilton College
128. Hamline University (Minnesota)
129. Hampden-Sydney College
130. Hampshire College
131. Hanover College
132. Hartwick College
133. Harvard University

THE NINTH-GRADE GUIDE FOR INVOLVED PARENTS

134. Harvey Mudd College
135. Haverford College
136. Hendrix College
137. Hillsdale College
138. Hiram College
139. Hobart and William Smith Colleges
140. Hofstra University
141. Hollins University
142. Hood College
143. Hope College
144. Howard University
145. Husson University
146. Illinois College
147. Illinois Institute of Technology
148. Illinois Wesleyan University
149. Immaculata University
150. Iona College
151. Ithaca College
152. Jacobs University Bremen
153. John Cabot University in Rome
154. John Carroll University
155. Johns Hopkins University
156. Johnson State College
157. Juniata College
158. Kalamazoo College
159. Keene State College
160. Kenyon College
161. Keystone College
162. King's College
163. Knox College
164. Lafayette College
165. Lake Erie College
166. Lake Forest College

Appendix 6—Institutions Accepting the Common Application

167. La Salle University
168. Lasell College
169. Lawrence Technological University
170. Lawrence University
171. Lehigh University
172. Le Moyne College
173. Lesley College
174. Lewis & Clark College
175. Linfield College
176. Lipscomb University
177. List College The Jewish Theological Seminary
178. Long Island University Brooklyn Campus
179. Long Island University - C.W. Post Campus
180. Loyola Marymount University
181. Loyola University Maryland
182. Loyola University New Orleans
183. Luther College
184. Lycoming College
185. Lyndon State College
186. Lynn University
187. Macalester College
188. Manhattan College
189. Manhattanville College
190. Marietta College
191. Marist College
192. Marlboro College
193. Marquette University
194. Marymount Manhattan College
195. Maryville University of St. Louis
196. Massachusetts College of Pharmacy and Health Sciences
197. McDaniel College
198. Menlo College
199. Mercyhurst College

THE NINTH-GRADE GUIDE FOR INVOLVED PARENTS

200. Meredith College
201. Merrimack College
202. Miami University (Ohio)
203. Middlebury College
204. Millsaps College
205. Mills College
206. Moravian College
207. Morehouse College
208. Mount Holyoke College
209. Mount Saint Mary College
210. Mount St. Mary's College
211. Muhlenberg College
212. Naropa University
213. Nazareth College
214. Newbury College
215. New College of Florida
216. New England College
217. New School - Eugene Lang College
218. New York Institute of Technology (NYIT)
219. New York University
220. Niagara University
221. Nichols College
222. Northeastern University
223. Northland College
224. Northwestern University
225. Notre Dame de Namur University
226. Notre Dame of Maryland University
227. Oberlin College
228. Occidental College
229. Oglethorpe University
230. Ohio Northern University
231. Ohio Wesleyan University
232. Oklahoma City University

Appendix 6—Institutions Accepting the Common Application

233. Otterbein University
234. Pace University
235. Pacific Lutheran University
236. Pacific University
237. Pepperdine University
238. Philadelphia University
239. Pitzer College
240. Plymouth State University
241. Polytechnic Institute of New York University
242. Pomona College
243. Presbyterian College
244. Prescott College
245. Princeton University
246. Providence College
247. Quinnipiac University
248. Ramapo College of New Jersey
249. Randolph College
250. Randolph-Macon College
251. Reed College
252. Regis College
253. Regis University
254. Rensselaer Polytechnic Institute
255. Rhode Island College
256. Rhodes College
257. Rice University
258. Richard Stockton College of New Jersey
259. Rider University
260. Ringling College of Art and Design
261. Ripon College
262. Rochester Institute of Technology
263. Roger Williams University
264. Rollins College
265. Rosemont College

THE NINTH-GRADE GUIDE FOR INVOLVED PARENTS

266. Russell Sage College
267. Sacred Heart University
268. Sage College of Albany
269. Saint Anselm College
270. Saint Francis University
271. Saint John's University (College of Saint Benedict)
272. Saint Joseph's College of Maine
273. Saint Joseph's University
274. Saint Leo University
275. Saint Louis University
276. Saint Martin's University
277. Saint Mary's College of California
278. Saint Mary's College of Indiana
279. Saint Mary's University of Minnesota
280. Saint Michael's College
281. Saint Peter's College
282. Saint Vincent College
283. Salem College
284. Salisbury University
285. Salve Regina University
286. Samford University
287. Santa Clara University
288. Sarah Lawrence College
289. School of the Art Institute of Chicago
290. Scripps College
291. Seattle Pacific University
292. Seattle University
293. Seton Hall University
294. Seton Hill University
295. Sewanee: The University of the South
296. Siena College
297. Sierra Nevada College
298. Simmons College

Appendix 6—Institutions Accepting the Common Application

299. Skidmore College
300. Smith College
301. Southern Methodist University
302. Southern New Hampshire University
303. Southwestern University
304. Spelman College
305. Spring Hill College
306. Stanford University
307. St. Bonaventure University
308. St. Catherine University
309. St. Edward's University
310. Stephens College
311. Stetson University
312. Stevens Institute of Technology
313. Stevenson University
314. St. John Fisher College
315. St. John's College (MD)
316. St. John's College (NM)
317. St. Joseph's College - Brooklyn Campus
318. St. Joseph's College - Long Island Campus
319. St. Lawrence University
320. St. Mary's College of Maryland
321. St. Norbert College
322. St. Olaf College
323. Stonehill College
324. St. Thomas Aquinas College
325. Suffolk University
326. SUNY Binghamton University
327. SUNY Buffalo State College
328. SUNY College at Brockport
329. SUNY College at Geneseo
330. SUNY College at Old Westbury
331. SUNY College at Oneonta

THE NINTH-GRADE GUIDE FOR INVOLVED PARENTS

332. SUNY College of Environmental Science & Forestry
333. SUNY Cortland
334. SUNY Fredonia
335. SUNY Institute of Technology
336. SUNY Maritime College
337. SUNY Morrisville State College
338. SUNY New Paltz
339. SUNY Oswego
340. SUNY Plattsburgh
341. SUNY Potsdam
342. SUNY Purchase College
343. SUNY Stony Brook University
344. SUNY University at Albany
345. SUNY University at Buffalo
346. Susquehanna University
347. Swarthmore College
348. Sweet Briar College
349. Syracuse University
350. Texas Christian University
351. The American University of Paris
352. The American University of Rome
353. The Catholic University of America
354. The College of Idaho
355. The College of New Jersey
356. The College of New Rochelle
357. The College of Saint Rose
358. The George Washington University
359. The University of Scranton
360. The University of Tulsa
361. Thiel College
362. Thomas College
363. Towson University
364. Transylvania University

Appendix 6—Institutions Accepting the Common Application

365. Trinity College
366. Trinity University
367. Tufts University
368. Union College
369. University of Chicago
370. University of Connecticut
371. University of Dallas
372. University of Dayton
373. University of Delaware
374. University of Denver
375. University of Evansville
376. University of Findlay
377. University of Great Falls
378. University of Hartford
379. University of Kentucky
380. University of LaVerne
381. University of Maine
382. University of Maine at Farmington
383. University of Maine at Machias
384. University of Maryland, Baltimore County
385. University of Mary Washington
386. University of Massachusetts Amherst
387. University of Massachusetts Boston
388. University of Massachusetts Dartmouth
389. University of Massachusetts Lowell
390. University of Miami
391. University of Michigan
392. University of New England
393. University of New Hampshire
394. University of New Haven
395. University of New Orleans
396. University of North Carolina Asheville
397. University of North Carolina at Chapel Hill

THE NINTH-GRADE GUIDE FOR INVOLVED PARENTS

398. University of North Carolina at Wilmington
399. University of Notre Dame
400. University of Pennsylvania
401. University of Portland
402. University of Puget Sound
403. University of Redlands
404. University of Rhode Island
405. University of Richmond
406. University of Rochester
407. University of San Diego
408. University of San Francisco
409. University of Southern California
410. University of Southern Maine
411. University of St Andrews
412. University of Tampa
413. University of the Pacific
414. University of the Sciences
415. University of Vermont
416. University of Virginia
417. Ursinus College
418. Utica College
419. Valparaiso University
420. Vanderbilt University
421. Vassar College
422. Villanova University
423. Wabash College
424. Wagner College
425. Wake Forest University
426. Wartburg College
427. Washington and Lee University
428. Washington College
429. Washington & Jefferson College
430. Washington University in St. Louis

Appendix 6—Institutions Accepting the Common Application

431. Webster University
432. Wellesley College
433. Wells College
434. Wentworth Institute of Technology
435. Wesleyan University
436. Western New England University
437. Westminster College (Missouri)
438. Westminster College (Pennsylvania)
439. Westminster College (Utah)
440. Westmont College
441. Wheaton College
442. Wheeling Jesuit University
443. Wheelock College
444. Whitman College
445. Whittier College
446. Whitworth University
447. Willamette University
448. William Jewell College
449. Williams College
450. Wilson College
451. Wittenberg University
452. Wofford College
453. Worcester Polytechnic Institute
454. Xavier University
455. Xavier University of Louisiana
456. Yale University

© 2011 The Common Application, Inc. Reprinted with permission.

References

ACT.org, National Collegiate Retention. Retrieved June 17, 2010 from: *www.act.org/research/policymakers/pdf/retain_2009.pdf*

Alsop, Ron. (October 21, 2008). The Trophy Kids Grow Up: How the Millennial Generation Is Shaking Up the Workplace" WSJ. Retrieved June 17, 2010 from: http://online.wsj.com/article/SB122455219391652725.html.

Bronson, Po. (February 12, 2007). How not to talk to your kids. *New York Magazine*. Retrieved July 22, 2008 from: *http://nymag.com/news/features/27840/*.

Bruns, Jerome. 1992. *They can but they don't: Helping students overcome work inhibition.* New York: Penguin.

CommonApp.org. Teacher Evaluation. Retrieved February 26, 2012 from: *www.commonapp.org/CommonApp/docs/downloadforms/Teacher_Evaluation.pdf*.

Duckworth, Angela L. and Seligman, Martin E. P. (2005). Self-discipline outdoes IQ in predicting academic performance of adolescents. *Psychological Science 16* (12), 939–944. Retrieved March 1, 2007 from: *www.blackwell-synergy.com/doi/abs/*.

REFERENCES

Foss, Kathleen and Lathrop, Ann. (2000). *Student cheating and plagiarism in the Internet era: a wake-up call.* Englewood: Libraries Unlimited

NCHEMS Information Center. Retention Rate. Retrieved June 17, 2008 from: *http://www.higheredinfo.org/dbrowser/index.php?submeasure=223&year=2008&level=nation&mode=graph&state=0*

Rathvon, Natalie.(1996). *The unmotivated child.* New York: Fireside.

Spiegel, Alix. (February 21, 2008). Old-fashioned play builds serious skills. NPR. Retrieved July 1, 2008 from: *www.npr.org/templates/story/story.php?storyId=19212514.*

Walsh, David. (2004). *Why do they act that way?* New York: Free Press.

Wolf, Anthony. (1996). *Get out of my life but first could you drive me and Cheryl to the mall?* New York: LLC

THE NINTH-GRADE GUIDE FOR INVOLVED PARENTS

Ellen Shrager has been a community college instructor in Massachusetts and a high school teacher in New Hampshire. She is currently a full-time seventh-grade teacher in Pennsylvania.

Mrs. Shrager is a frequent keynote speaker at state and regional conferences, leads workshops and sessions at national conventions such as ASCD, ASCA, NMSA, and ACTFL, and has presented more than fifty school in-services for teachers and parents.

She talks about the top five changes in society, how they impact the way students are raised, and the behaviors and skills students bring to the classroom. She inspires teachers to build a bridge between where the children are and where they need to be to function in the classroom.

Mrs. Shrager also talks about the top five changes in society that influence some parents to enable their children. She helps teachers to discern parental illusions and engage in dialogues with parents in such a way that the parents support appropriate consequences for their children's behavior and effort.

Ellen understands that parents can't do this in a vacuum. Her wish is to help ninth-grade parents to **unite** to let their children accept natural consequences. She suggests:

ABOUT THE AUTHOR

- ♥ Professional school counselors sponsor a Parent Education Series to discuss the book and support one another.

- ♥ Parent Teacher Association (PTO, PTA, ATP) sponsor a book club to discuss the book and support one another.

- ♥ Eighth-grade parents form a book club to prepare for ninth grade.

- ♥ Pediatricians and nurse practitioners encourage parents to share this book with the parents of their children's friends.

- ♥ Wellness directors encourage employees with children in ninth grade to form a support group to help one another to have their children accept natural consequences.

- ♥ Librarians run a book club to help parents and grandparents encourage natural consequences.

- ♥ Professional school counselors use the information in this book to present to faculty members for staff development.

To help start a support group, or to share your experiences, contact Ellen Shrager at teachervoicepublishing@comcast.net.

She is currently working on the fourth edition of her book **Teacher Dialogues.** She lives in Newtown Square, Pennsylvania, with her husband, Ed.

THE NINTH-GRADE GUIDE FOR INVOLVED PARENTS

TO ORDER, OR FOR MORE INFORMATION ON VOLUME DISCOUNTS, CALL
1 (610) 355-0553
E-MAIL: teachervoicepublishing@comcast.net
P.O. BOX 446   VILLANOVA, PA 19085-0446

TEACHER DIALOGUES	$20
THE NINTH-GRADE GUIDE FOR INVOLVED PARENTS	$20
THE INVOLVED PARENT'S SIXTH GRADE GUIDE	$20
THE INVOLVED PARENT'S SEVENTH GRADE GUIDE	$20
FOUR MINUTES A DAY	$14
THE WORLD LANGUAGE DAILY TECH GUIDE	$20
STUDENT PERFORMANCE CHART	$3
A-C-T- POSTER	$3
A-C-T- REMINDER CARD	$1
AFTERNOON/EVENING HABITS CARD	$1
PROJECT CARD	$1
IN-CLASS HABITS CARD	$1

A SCHOOL GUIDE
TO IDENTIFYING AND NEUTRALIZING
"ENTERTAINMENT BULLYING"

FOUR MINUTES A DAY

A PARENT AND TEACHER SURVIVAL GUIDE FOR VICTIMS OF "ENTERTAINMENT BULLYING" IN SCHOOL HALLWAYS

by E. C. Bernard

A BLUEPRINT FOR PROTECTING THE VICTIMS OF BULLYING WITH ADVICE FOR PARENTS, TEACHERS, AND SCHOOL ADMINISTRATORS

"My son has been the target of constant teasing starting from the first day of 7th grade. I can't even tell you how much stress and strain the teasing has placed on our family. We were really at a breaking point emotionally. The FOUR MINUTES A DAY project has literally changed his whole perception of school now and has changed our lives at home. He no longer walks in the door from school crying and hating school. He is actually happy." a mother

"Before this alliance was formed, I thought I would have lost hope. Kids were constantly teasing me ... and I was even considering missing school! Once you stepped in with this program, those problems were vanquished and done with. I feel safer now that I walk with students in the halls. Plus, I am even starting to make new friends. Thanks a ton for starting The FOUR MINUTES A DAY project." a 7th grader

"I realized the little things in life one may do, can make a big difference in someone else's life." a student volunteer

WITH GROUNDBREAKING INSIGHT INTO BULLYING, E.C. BERNARD OFFERS A PROVEN SOLUTION TO BULLIED STUDENTS FEELING ISOLATED AND AFRAID IN SCHOOL HALLWAYS.

ISBN 978-0-9793200-7-1

Teacher Dialogues

by
Ellen Shrager

Third Printing

A Survival Guide to Successful Dialogues with

Low-Performing Students
Indulged Students
Enabling Parents
Cross-Generational Colleagues

Illustrated by Abby Bosley
and Anthony T. Shelton, Sr.

Dear Colleagues,

As I enter my 25th year of teaching, many changes in society continue to impact my classroom delivery in three ways:

❤ STUDENTS - Five fundamental changes in society influence undesirable behaviors children bring to school. Learn how to build a bridge between where students are and where they need to be in order to function appropriately in the classroom. (See page 59.)

❤ PARENTS - Five different changes in society influence some parents to enable their children. Learn how to listen to enabling parents, discern their illusions, and compassionately offer facts to guide them to support appropriate consequences for their children's behavior and efforts. (See page 117.)

❤ CROSS-GENERATIONAL COLLEAGUES - Similar changes contribute to miscommunication among the cross-generational teaching staff. There are ten implicit rules of conduct that should be made explicit, and can be the springboard for discussion for faculty meetings and for mentor meetings with new teachers. (See page 82)

What we teachers learned in our teacher preparatory courses represent the border of a large jigsaw puzzle — this book will help fill in the missing pieces.

Sincerely,
Ellen Shrager

THE WORLD LANGUAGE
DAILY TECH GUIDE
by Ellen Shrager

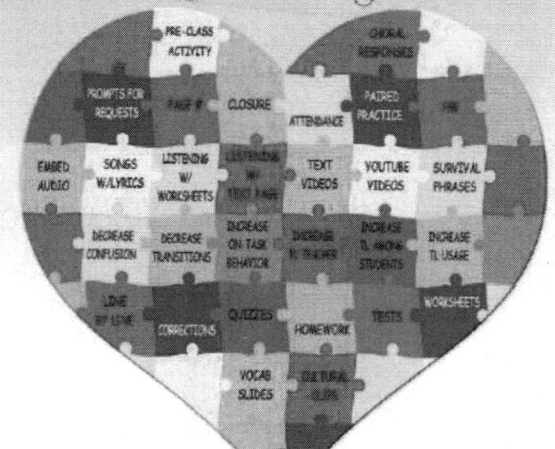

A Survival Guide to Using Technology
to Improve Classroom Management
and to Visually Support
the 90% Target Language Goal
for Level One Students
at the Secondary Level